H[illegible] Thanksgiving!

by Wiley Blevins

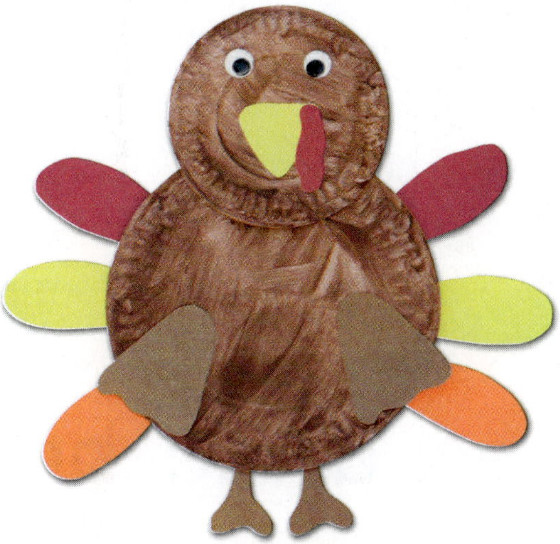

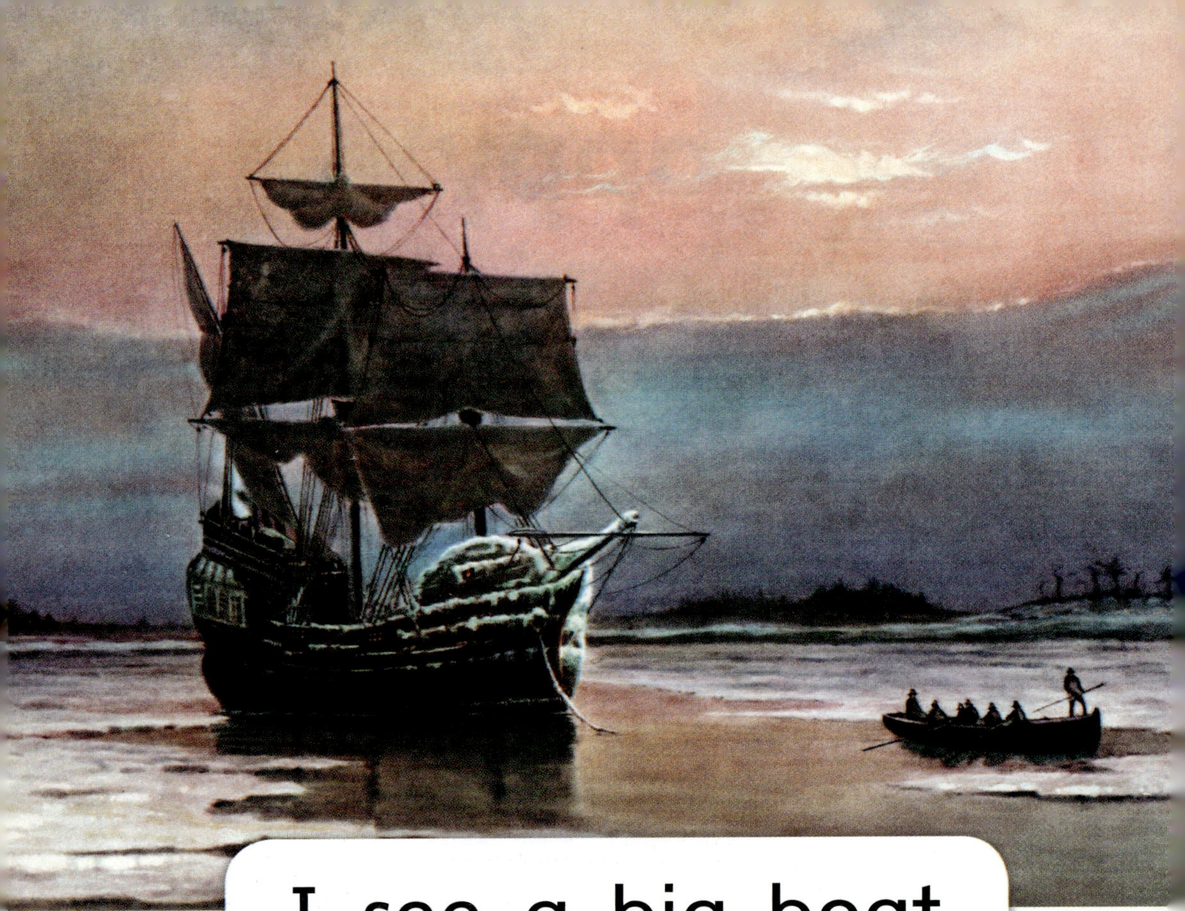

I see a big boat.

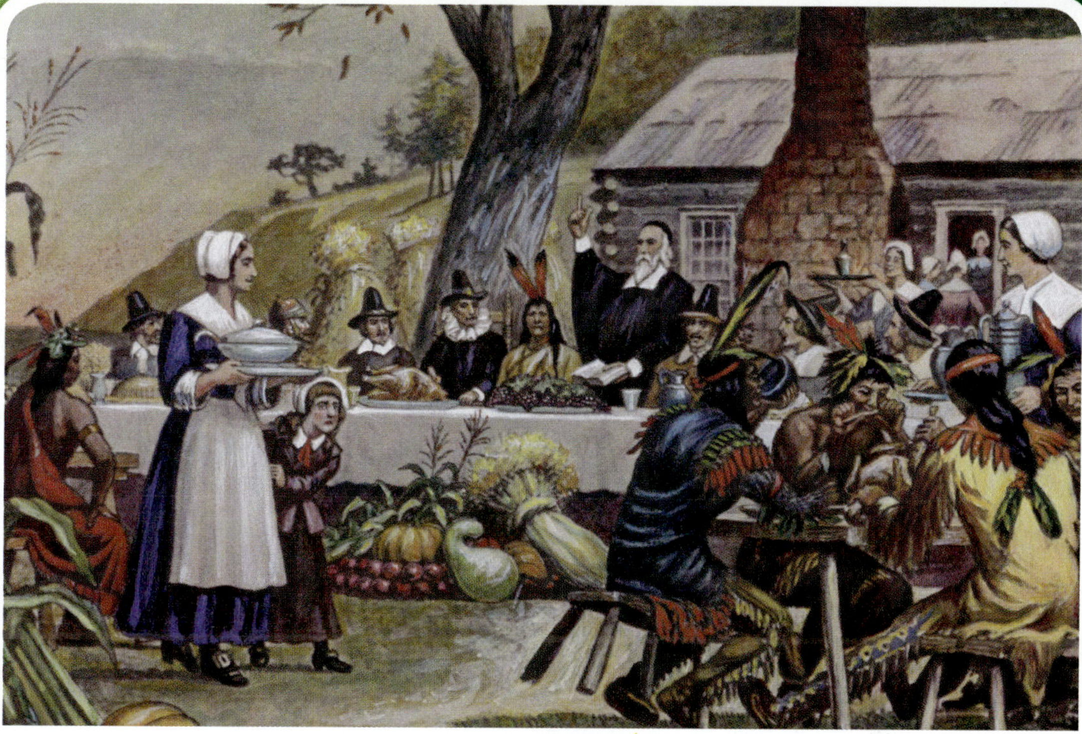

I see a big meal.

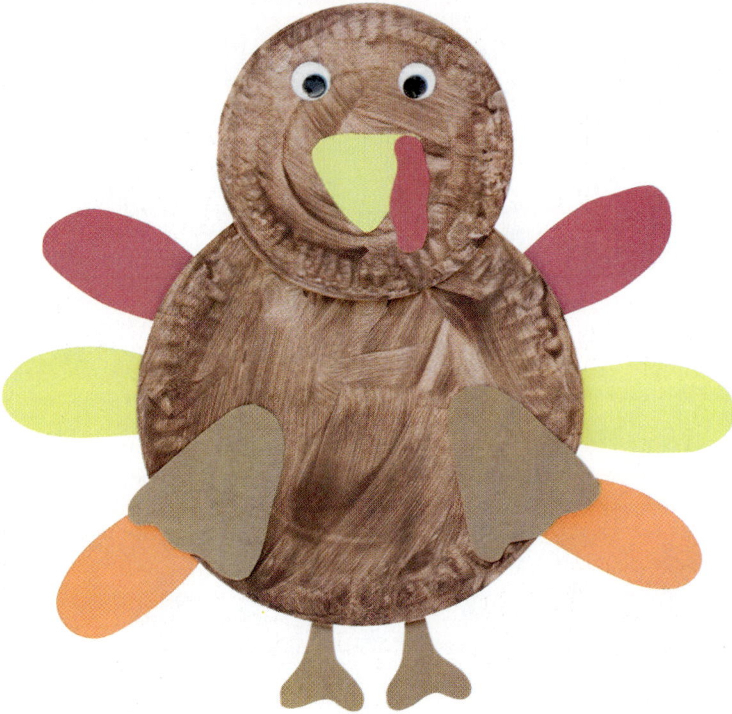

I see a big turkey.

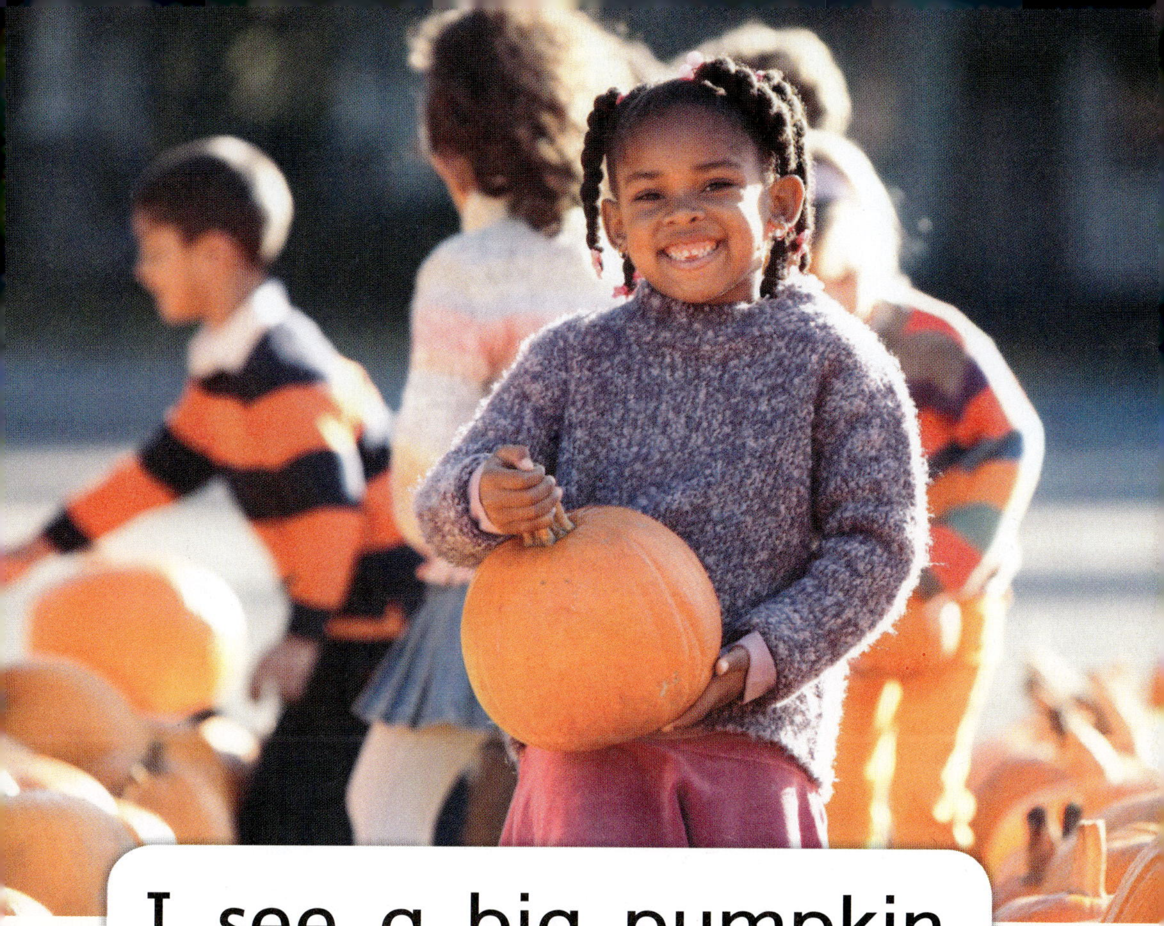

I see a big pumpkin.

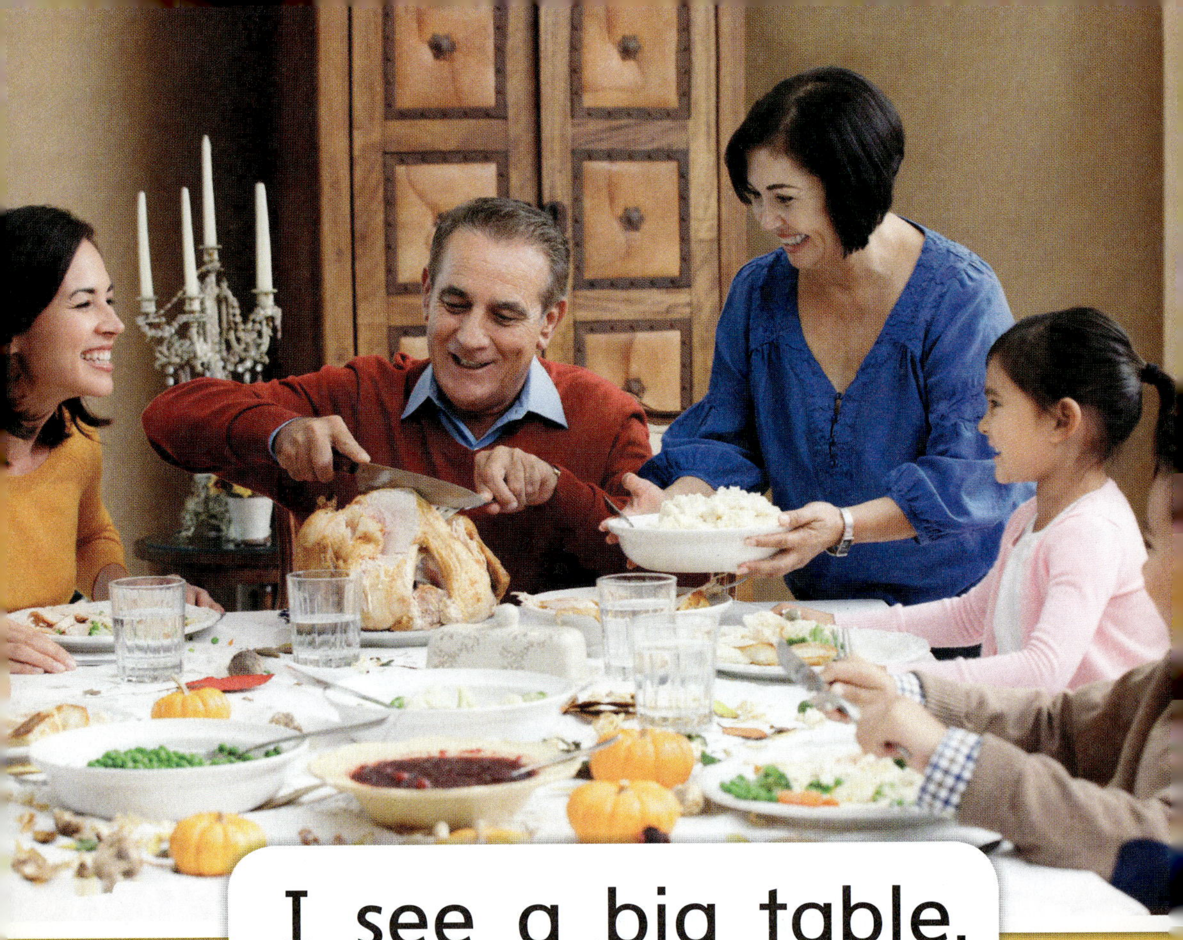

I see a big table.

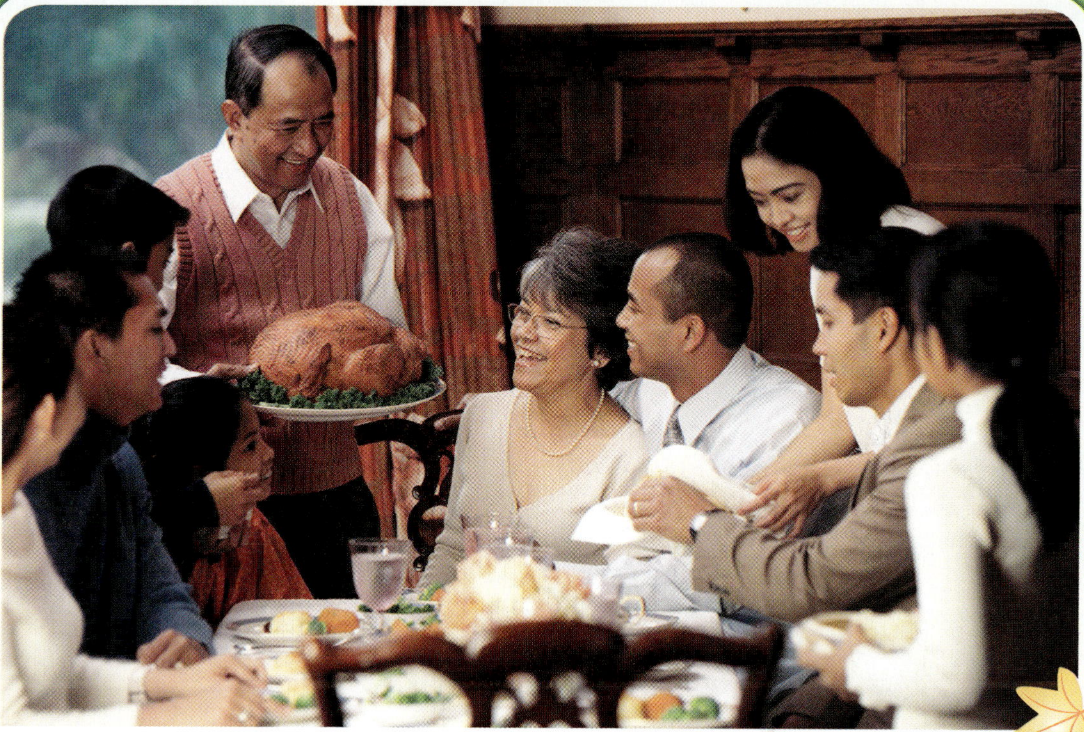

I see a big family.

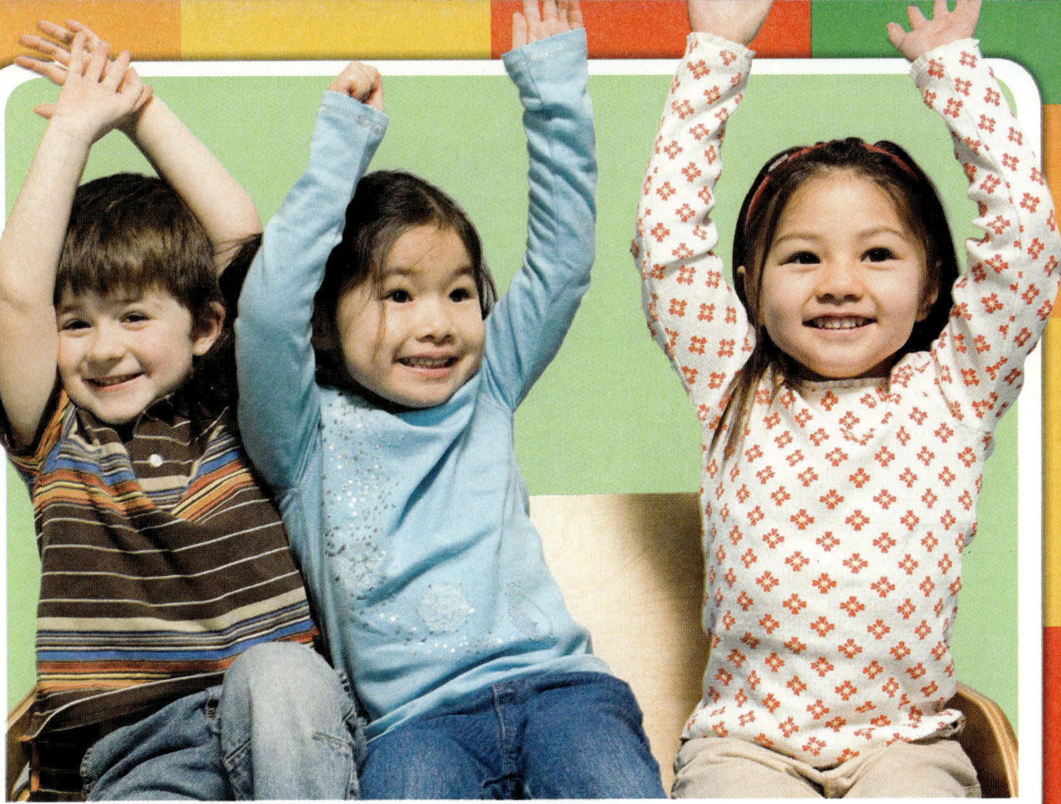

Happy Thanksgiving!